© 2013 Owlkids Books Inc.
10 Lower Spadina Avenue, Suite 400, Toronto, Ontario M5V 2Z2
www.owlkidsbooks.com

Text by the Editors of *Chirp Magazine*
Illustrations by Bob Kain

Distributed in Canada by University of Toronto Press
5201 Dufferin Street, Toronto, Ontario M3H 5T8

Distributed in the United States by Publishers Group West
1700 Fourth Street, Berkeley, California 94710

Library and Archives Canada Cataloguing in Publication

     Joking around with Chirp / by the editors of Chirp magazine ; illustrated
by Bob Kain.

ISBN 978-1-926973-64-7 (bound).--ISBN 978-1-926973-65-4 (pbk.)

     1. Wit and humor, Juvenile. 2. Riddles, Juvenile. 3. Tongue twisters.
I. Kain, Bob, 1932- II. Title: Chirp (Toronto, Ont.)

PN6371.5.J65 2013   j818'.602   C2012-905419-4

Library of Congress Control Number: 2012948719

Design: Barb Kelly

Canadian Heritage   Patrimoine canadien   **Canadä**   **Ontario**
Ontario Media Development Corporation

Canada Council for the Arts   Conseil des Arts du Canada   **ONTARIO ARTS COUNCIL CONSEIL DES ARTS DE L'ONTARIO**   Société de développement de l'industrie des médias de l'Ontario

We acknowledge the financial support of the Canada Council for the Arts, the Ontario Arts
Council, the Government of Canada through the Canada Book Fund (CBF) and the Government
of Ontario through the Ontario Media Development Corporation's Book Initiative for our
publishing activities.

Manufactured by WKT Co. Ltd.
Manufactured in Shenzhen, Guangdong, China, in October 2012
Job #12CB1763

A   B   C   D   E   F

Publisher of Chirp, chickaDEE and OWL
www.owlkidsbooks.com

Joking Around with Chirp

HEE HEE   HA HA

More Than 130 Feather-Ruffling Jokes, Riddles, and Tongue Twisters!

Owl kids

What do frogs play at recess?

Leapfrog.

What kind of house makes chirping sounds?
A birdhouse.
What game do birds like to play?
Hide-and-beak.
What did the little bird say to the big bird?
"Peck on someone your own size."
Why do hummingbirds hum?
Because they don't know the words.

What do you call a lazy kangaroo?

A pouch potato.

What's the difference between a cookie and a penguin?

You can't dunk a penguin in a glass of milk.

What do you get if you cross a worm with a gorilla?

Very big holes in your garden.

Knock, knock.
Who's there?
Lettuce.
Lettuce who?
Lettuce in, we're hungry!

What does a turtle do on its birthday?

It shell-ebrates.

What do you call a sleeping bull?

A bulldozer.

What is green and can jump a mile a minute?

A grasshopper with the hiccups.

What do you get when you cross a tiger with a sheep?

A striped sweater.

What did the cowboy say when he fell off his horse?

"I've fallen and I can't giddy-up!"

What do you call a sick alligator?

An ill-igator.

What do astronauts do when they get dirty?

They take a
meteor shower.

Say this 5 times fast:
Funny fish face

Why can't you play games in grasslands?

There are too many cheat-ahs.

Why did the baby chicken cross the playground?

To get to the other slide.

What do elephants bring on vacation?

Their trunks.

Say this 5 times fast:
Four flying feathered friends

Knock, knock.

Who's there?

House.

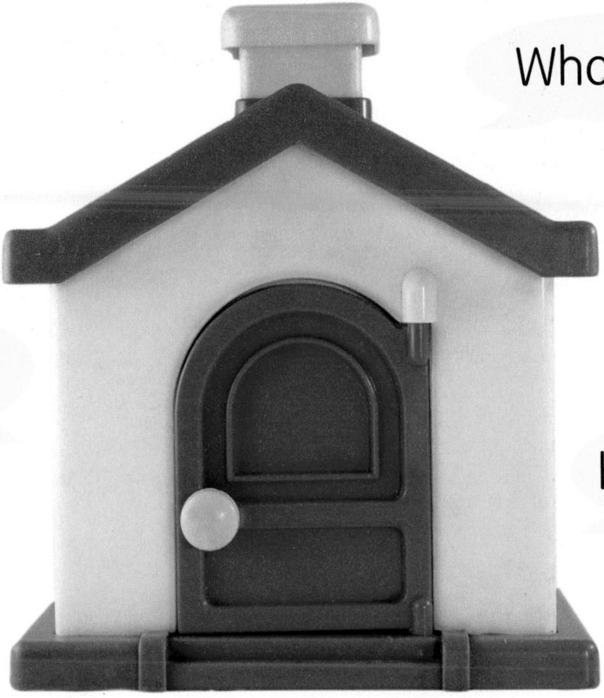

House who?

House it going?

What do polar bears eat for lunch?

Iceberg-ers.

What did the lighthouse say to the ocean?

"Sea you later."

What's a frog's favorite food?

French flies.

Why did the stegosaurus wear a bandage?

It had a dino-sore.

HEE HEE...

HA
HA

What do you call a dinosaur that likes to jump rope?

A hop-o-saurus.

What do you call an alligator that skates?

A gator skater.

What kind of monkey flies?

A hot-air baboon.

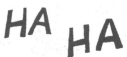 HA HA

What do you get if you cross a skunk with a vegetable?

Smell-ery.

HA
HA

What is the wettest animal?

The rain-deer.

Why did the bear tiptoe past the campers?

It didn't want to wake up the sleeping bags.

HA

HA
HA

Say this 5 times fast:
Baby baboon

How can you tell if an elephant's been in your fridge?

Footprints in the butter.

What do you call a rooster that wakes you up in the morning?

An alarm cluck.

Say this 5 times fast:
Dining dinosaur

For eating potato chips in bed.

Where do sharks go on vacation?

The Shark-tic.

Why didn't the lobster share its toys?

Because it was shellfish.

What fish swims at night?

A starfish.

Why don't octopuses like dinnertime?

They have too many hands to wash before they can eat.

What happens
when ducks fly
upside down?

They quack up.

What happened to the cat who ate the yarn?

She had a litter of mittens.

What do you call a camel in the Arctic?

Lost.

Say this 5 times fast:
Awesome airplane

Why did the lamb say "moo"?

It was learning a new language.

What's a monster's favorite cheese?

Monster-ella.

What do you call a hungry vampire?

Snack-ula.

What do you give a monster for its birthday?

Anything it wants.

What does a vampire bathe in?

A bat-tub.

What's a monster's favorite drink?

Ghoul-ade.

Why do mummies make excellent spies?

They're good at keeping things under wraps.

What's Dracula's favorite fruit?

Neck-tarines.

What do monsters like to eat?

Ice scream.

Why do spiders spin webs?

Because they don't know how to knit.

What do toads drink at picnics?

Croak-a-Cola.

What fruit do gorillas like?

Ape-ricots.

Say this 5 times fast:
Marvelous music

What do you call a cow that cuts grass?

A lawn mooer.

What do you call a baby elephant that needs a bath?

A smelly-phant.

What did the bee say to the flower?

How do bees get to school?

"Hello, honey!"

What did the bee say to the honey?

"I'm stuck on you."

They ride the school buzz.

Why do bees have sticky hair?

Because they use honeycombs.

What game do bees like to play?

Fris-bee.

Say this 5 times fast:
Dancing daisies

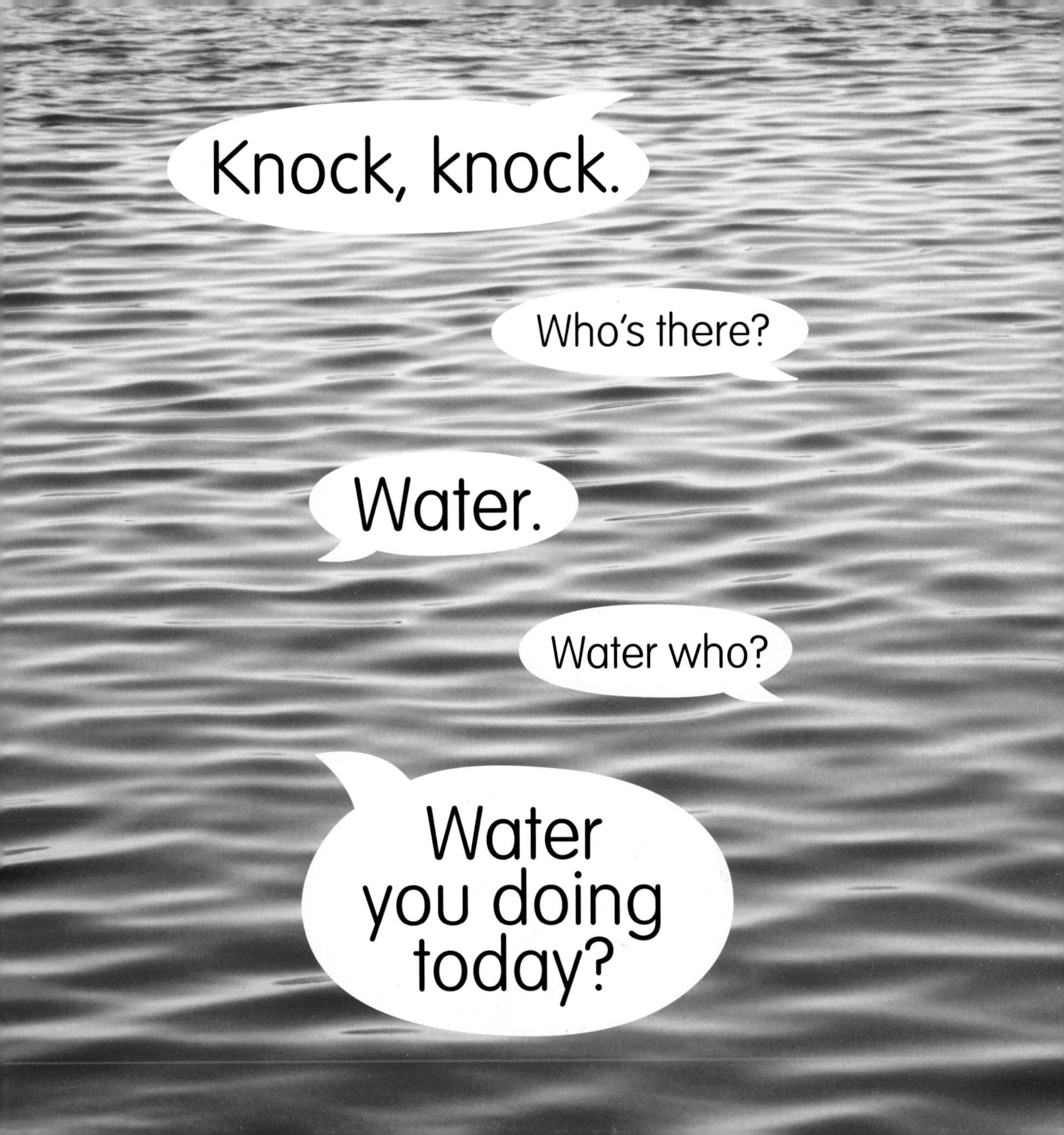
Knock, knock.
Who's there?
Water.
Water who?
Water you doing today?

What do you call a cat that's afraid of a ghost?

A scaredy-cat.

What is the strongest animal of all?

A snail—it carries around its own house!

What did one tornado say to the other?

"Let's twist again."

HA
HA

What kind of tree can you hold in your hand?

A palm tree.

What kind of bow is impossible to tie?

A rainbow.

HA HA

What is a tree's favorite drink?

Root beer.

HA
HA

What's louder than a cat stuck in a tree?

Two cats stuck in a tree.

HA
HA
HA
HA

When does a vet need an umbrella?

When it rains cats and dogs.

What kind of dog has the cleanest fur?

A shampoo-dle.

On what day do lions eat?

Chews-day.

Where do polar bears go on vacation?

Bear-muda.

Say this 5 times fast:
Super snow

Where do ghosts get their mail?

The ghost office.

What does a witch get in a hotel?

Broom service.

What is a ghost's favorite food?

Boo-loney.

How do skeletons call their friends?

On the tele-bone.

How do goblins like to travel?

On fright trains.

What is a ghost's favorite candy?

Boo-ble gum.

Why do witches fly on brooms?

Because vacuum cleaners are too heavy.

What did the ghost do when it got in its car?

It buckled its sheet-belt.

What kind of dog has no tail?

A hot dog.

What's worse than finding a worm in your apple?

Finding half a worm in your apple.

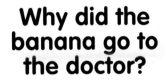

Why did the banana go to the doctor?

It wasn't peeling well.

Why don't bananas ever get lonely?

Because they hang around in bunches.

Why did the banana use sunscreen?

So it wouldn't peel.

How do you know carrots are good for your eyes?

You never see rabbits wearing glasses.